W9-APL-883

Great Careers for People Fascinated by
Government & the Law

by
Anne Marie Males

contributing authors
Julie Czerneda
and
Victoria Vincent

An imprint of Gale Research,
An ITP Information/Reference Group Company

Changing the Way the World Learns

NEW YORK • LONDON • BONN • BOSTON • DETROIT • MADRID
MELBOURNE • MEXICO CITY • PARIS • SINGAPORE • TOKYO
TORONTO • WASHINGTON • ALBANY NY • BELMONT CA • CINCINNATI OH

© 1996
Trifolium Books Inc. and Weigl Educational Publishers Limited

First published in Canada by Trifolium Books Inc. and Weigl Educational Publishers Limited

U•X•L is the exclusive publisher of the U.S. library edition of Series 3.

An imprint of
Gale Research
835 Penobscot Bldg.
Detroit, MI 48226

Library of Congress Catalog Card Number 95-62265
ISBN 0-7876-0858-0

The activities in this book have been tested and are safe when carried out as suggested. The publishers can accept no responsibility for any damage caused or sustained by use or misuse of ideas or materials mentioned within.

Acknowledgments
The author and the publishers wish to thank those people whose careers are featured in this book for allowing us to interview and photograph them at work. Their love for their chosen careers has made our task an enjoyable one.

Design concept: Julian Cleva
Design and layout: Warren Clark, Karen Dudley
Editors: Ann Downar, Rosemary Tanner, Julie Czerneda
Project coordinator, proofreader: Diane Klim
Production coordinator: Amanda Woodrow
Content review: Gillian Bartlett, Trudy Rising

Printed and bound in Canada
10 9 8 7 6 5 4 3 2 1

This book's text stock contains more than 50% recycled paper.

Contents

Featured profiles

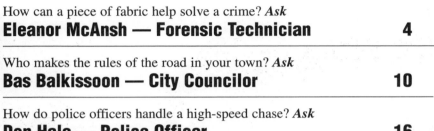

How can a piece of fabric help solve a crime? *Ask*
Eleanor McAnsh — Forensic Technician   **4**

Who makes the rules of the road in your town? *Ask*
Bas Balkissoon — City Councilor   **10**

How do police officers handle a high-speed chase? *Ask*
Don Hale — Police Officer   **16**

How can a librarian be a detective? *Ask*
Ester Wan — Law Librarian   **22**

Who decides whether a student should be expelled? *Ask*
Jeff Kendall — School Board Trustee   **28**

Who represents your country in other countries? *Ask*
Lisa Stadelbauer — Foreign Service Officer   **34**

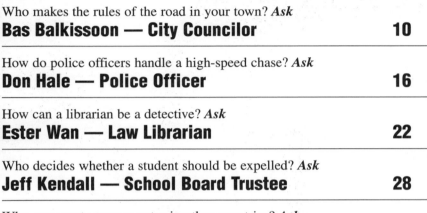

Careers at a glance

How can young offenders turn their lives around? *Ask*
Crys Mantas — Probation Officer   **40**

Who prepares the evidence for a big court case? *Ask*
Robin Duke — Law Clerk   **41**

What kinds of problems do lawyers solve? *Ask*
Rob Pattison — Lawyer   **42**

Who puts words in other people's mouths? *Ask*
Ken McGaw — Speech Writer   **43**

Who got the job?   **45**

Index/Credits/Answers   **48**

Eleanor McAnsh

Forensic Technician

PERSONAL PROFILE

Career: Forensic technician. "I use science to help the police investigate crimes."

Interests: Volleyball, baseball, swimming, and basketball. "Any sport — I love them all."

Latest accomplishment: "Some of the tests I ran became very important evidence in a recent case. The suspect was found guilty. He might have gone free without my forensic testing."

Why I do what I do: "I feel a sense of accomplishment knowing that what I do is beneficial to society."

I am: Logical, curious, persistent. "I like to hang in there until I have answers."

What I wanted to be when I was in school: "I've always been interested in science and thought about being a doctor or a paramedic. I decided on this career after touring a forensic lab while I was a student."

What a forensic technician does

At a crime scene, investigators collect many different objects as evidence. These objects are sealed in bags and sent to a forensic lab for examination and testing. Eleanor McAnsh is a forensic technician. "In the lab, I examine the items the investigators send in order to answer their questions about them." Forensic tests can uncover information to help locate suspects, eliminate suspects, or provide important clues for investigators. "Sometimes what we find in the lab turns out to be the crucial evidence used in the trial," Eleanor says.

Looking for trace evidence

Eleanor works in the biology section of a forensic laboratory. Her job is to examine articles of clothing and other items for trace evidence. "The clothing you're wearing right now has collected tiny fibers and hairs from your surroundings," she explains. "You may have a pet, or have hugged someone this morning."

Eleanor looks for fibers or hairs left on a victim or at a crime scene. "If you know what to look for, these small bits can be very significant."

Clues that "match"

When the investigators bring evidence to the lab, they provide background information that guides Eleanor's work. "For example, they may bring in two blood-stained samples, and ask us to find out if both samples could have come from the same person, called a 'match.' Or they may have a suspect, and want to see if we can identify any of that person's hair from the crime scene."

A forensic scientist coordinates the different lab tests, and Eleanor and the other technicians run those tests. "When I've finished, I report my results to the scientist who explains them to the investigators. Depending on the case, the scientist may also explain the findings in court."

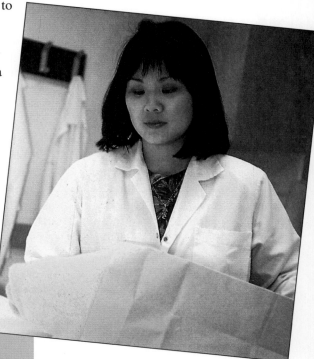

When Eleanor examines any piece of evidence, such as this sweater, she keeps careful notes. "Important information, such as date, procedures, and observations, must be accurately recorded."

Types of evidence

Anything found at a crime scene or on a suspect could be a valuable clue. For this reason, forensic science involves every area of science, from botany to physics. For example:

- Analysts in the **Documents** section examine handwriting samples and different kinds of paper. Many of their cases involve forgery.
- **Photography** analysts examine enhanced photographs of evidence to check for possible matches. For example, could a piece of headlight have come from a suspect's car?
- Technicians in **Biology** identify blood and other body fluids using DNA tests and other procedures. They also analyze hairs and fibers.
- In **Toxicology,** the technicians do blood alcohol and drug analyses.
- **Chemistry** technicians may identify paint fragments from hit-and-run traffic accidents. They can also tell if a car's headlights were on or off at the time of an accident.
- In **Firearms and Toolmarks**, analysts examine guns and tools. After a break-in, for example, they may test whether a particular crowbar was used.

It's a Fact

Forensic technicians compare paint samples from car manufacturers with chips of paint found after a hit-and-run accident. A tiny trace of paint can point to the make, year, and model of the vehicle involved.

All in a day's work

Eleanor's typical day starts in the morning. "We work regular office hours, unless something is needed more quickly. Then we may work late.

"On TV, when the police find evidence, they send it to the lab and have the results in a couple of hours. It just doesn't work that way in real life," she admits. "Although it would be nice. The tests take time to do properly — sometimes weeks — and you can't rush something that is this important." On the other hand, the investigators and prosecutors need the forensic results in order to proceed. "We do our best to get the job done quickly."

Examining evidence

Today, Eleanor is examining a victim's sweater from a crime scene. "When I start a new case, the first thing I do is read the case history. The investigator on the case suggests some tests, such as a blood or fiber examination," she explains. "This information gives me an idea of where to start."

The investigator has asked for a fiber test on the sweater. "So my next step is to collect any fibers," Eleanor says. She covers the entire garment with standard cellophane tape. "Not surprisingly, the technique is called taping! It's not high-tech, but it works just fine." Any loose fibers stick to the tape. "If any look like they might have come from the suspect's clothing, I remove them with forceps and mount them on a microscope slide."

Double vision

Eleanor examines the mounted fibers under a "comparison microscope." "This microscope looks a bit like binoculars. It has two sets of lenses, so I can view two different slides at the same time." She puts a slide with sample fibers from the suspect's clothing on one side of the microscope. On the other side, she places a slide of a fiber found on the sweater. "Looking at them both, it appears that they match. That is, the color, shape, and size of the fibers are similar. This evidence suggests that the two people were together. It's nearly impossible to be in close contact with someone and not exchange some hairs or fibers from your clothing."

After comparing the slides, Eleanor runs other tests on the fibers. "Sometimes, I use a solvent to remove the dye from the fibers," she explains. "Then, I test the dye from the suspect's garment and the unknown fiber to see if they behave the same under certain conditions."

Here, Eleanor starts to "tape" the sweater.

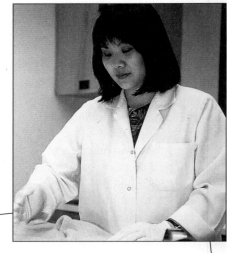

This graph shows the results of a test to measure the amount of light absorbed by three similar-looking red cotton fibers. "The red dye in each fiber absorbed light slightly differently," Eleanor explains. "This tells me that the fibers likely came from different sources, rather than the same piece of clothing."

Absorbance

1.0

0.8

0.4

400.0   450.0   500.0   550.0   600.0   650.0   nm

——— Red cotton #1
• • • • • • Red cotton $2
— — — Red cotton #3

Lab routine

Eleanor spends most of her day running tests and recording her results. "The tests won't mean anything if my records aren't accurate and complete," she cautions.

Evidence must be repacked and stored. "It may be months before a trial actually takes place, so every piece of evidence, from paper to a sofa, has to be stored where it can't be tampered with or damaged by the weather."

She pauses and looks very serious.

"Everything I do in this lab is part of the legal process. And we never forget that our results could have a direct impact on someone's life, whether victim or suspect."

Conducting tests is meticulous, painstaking work. Technicians must be careful not to contaminate their evidence.

Levels of certainty

There is usually some uncertainty in forensic results, just as in other areas of science. "There's rarely anything that is one hundred percent certain," Eleanor agrees. "I may be able to match fibers, but because clothing is mass-produced, those fibers could have come from somewhere else."

Activity

Examining trace evidence

Eleanor relies on the technique of taping to help find evidence such as fiber or hair on fabric. You can try this technique for yourself in this activity.

You will need
- clear cellophane tape (such as packing tape)
- clear plastic (such as a page protector or plastic wrap)
- a microscope
- an article of clothing you wore this morning

Procedure
1. Apply a 10 cm piece of tape to the outside of your jacket, sweater, or shirt.
2. Remove the tape. Place it carefully on the clear sheet of plastic. This will seal any fibers or hairs in between.
3. Examine your tape carefully under a microscope. Sketch each of the different fibers and/or hairs you see. Make notes about the color and texture of each.
4. Where did each type of fiber or hair come from? How can you find out? Here are some suggestions from Eleanor.
- Obtain samples of fibers and hairs you suspect may be on your clothing, such as the fabric of the clothing itself and hair from your head. Examine these samples under the microscope. Compare them with your unknown samples and look for any that match.
- Hypothesize where other fibers and hairs may have come from, such as from the coat of the person next to you on the bus. How could you test this hypothesis?
- Record the characteristics of any fibers or hairs that remain unknown in a list. Take this list with you as you go through your day. Think about where you might have contacted the source of each. Be a detective!

How to become a forensic technician

Eleanor was interested in science in high school but didn't know what to do with her interest. "Then I took a tour of a forensic lab. That's what got me hooked," she says. She spoke to a forensic technician at the lab and received some good advice. "Because of the wide variety of tests performed in a forensic lab, many forensic technicians start by obtaining a degree in one particular area of science. So after high school, I studied biology and chemistry."

When Eleanor started there were few post-secondary programs specifically in forensic science. "I received my forensic training on the job," she recalls. "And I still do. Forensic science changes so quickly that you are always learning something new. The key is to have skill and experience handling scientific equipment. Most labs prefer to hire people with a strong science background. Then they teach you how to apply this knowledge forensically."

It's a Fact

Forensic technicians compare paint samples from car manufacturers with chips of paint found after a hit-and-run accident. A tiny trace of paint can point to the make, year, and model of the vehicle involved.

This display shows the methods used to identify a stain as human blood.

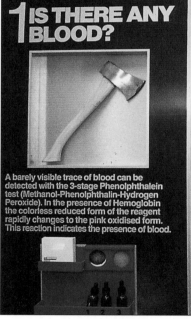

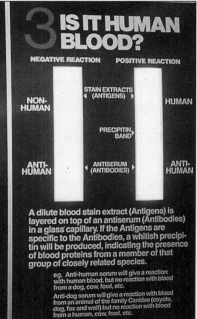

Is this career for you?

Most of the cases Eleanor works on are homicides or assaults. "We try not to get emotionally involved in the details of the crime," she explains. "You have to try and keep a certain detachment. There are lots of cases where children are involved. If you think too much about what happened, it would drive you crazy."

Regardless of the attention a case may receive, or how gruesome the crime, Eleanor believes the key is to be well-organized and to pay attention to detail. "There is no such thing as an unimportant test or procedure. Everything has to be done properly the first time." Good communication skills are also very helpful. "Absolutely," she agrees. "One minute I'm discussing my results with the scientist, the next I might be demonstrating a procedure to some police recruits. It helps to be a good listener — and to keep careful written notes."

Career planning

Making Career Connections

Visit the guidance office or library and ask for the addresses of universities or colleges that offer programs in forensic science. Write for information on how to enter such programs.

Call the science department of a college, university, or museum. Ask about the qualifications required to work as a lab technician. Find out if there are any summer or part-time opportunities available to high school students.

Some city police departments have small museums that show how crimes were solved over the years. Visit the museum and see how forensic science has changed.

Arrange to job shadow a lab technician in a hospital, veterinary clinic, or other lab. Take a notebook and keep a log of what the person does. What types of scientific equipment are used?

Getting started

Interested in being a forensic technician? Here's what you can do now.

1. Visit the science department head in your school and volunteer to help in the lab after school.
2. Join (or start) a science club.
3. If you have a chemistry set or microscope at home, learn how they work. Many experiments that you can conduct on your own are also used by technicians.
4. Read some of Sherlock Holmes' cases, by Sir Arthur Conan Doyle. This fictional detective relied on forensic techniques to solve mysteries. Write your own short story about Holmes, having him use scientific advances such as DNA testing.
5. In high school, take sciences and math. English courses will help you write good reports and communicate your results well.

Related careers

Here are some related careers you may want to check out.

Forensic scientist
Supervises a forensic lab. Presents and interprets evidence in court. Usually holds a post-graduate degree in one or more areas of science.

Pathologist
A physician who specializes in determining the causes of death. May visit the crime scene to do preliminary examinations.

Lab technician
Uses scientific methods and equipment for quality control, testing of unknowns, or other procedures. May work in industrial, government, medical, or research laboratories.

Archeologist
Investigates past civilizations. Uses scientific tests and analyses to find clues about how the people lived.

Future watch

"DNA-testing," Eleanor says firmly. "That's the big change taking place in forensic science." In DNA-testing, the genetic code of a suspect may be compared with that found in blood or tissue from a crime scene, for example. "Because each person's DNA is unique, it is a very powerful tool for investigators. All the scientists and technicians in our biology section are being trained in DNA-testing."

The future for this type of work? "Definitely expanding," says Eleanor. "Forensic science has become even more crucial to law enforcement. There's a strong need for well-trained technicians."

Bas Balkissoon

City Councilor

PERSONAL PROFILE

Career: City councilor. "A big part of my job is to act as a go-between for my community, representing their interests to the city staff."

Interests: Sports, especially soccer. "I'm very involved in coaching."

Latest accomplishment: "Controlling taxes has always been one of my goals. This year, there was no increase in taxes. I think I played a part in accomplishing that."

Why I do what I do: "I don't consider myself a politician, I consider myself a community representative. I'm here to change the things that upset many people about government."

I am: Good with people. "Listening is the key. Many people get frustrated because they don't feel they're being heard."

What I wanted to be when I was in school: "An electrician. I did become an electrician. Then, as I was promoted to floor manager and supervisor, this just seemed like a natural progression."

What a city councilor does

"A city council is like the board of directors for a big company," says Bas Balkissoon. "Our role is to make the final decisions on how tax money is spent and to deal with the concerns of the taxpayers." Bas has been a city councilor in a large North American city since his first election seven years ago.

City councilors are responsible for keeping the city running. "That includes everything from roads and traffic to land development," Bas says. While keeping within government regulations and laws, municipal governments like Bas' also decide how to do what the voters have asked. "You can think of this level of government as the get-to-work bunch," he jokes. "What we do — or don't do — our voters see right away."

Shaping the community

City councils have a lot to say about how a city is run. "We make decisions based on our regulations and laws, and, of course, the budget," explains Bas. "Say your community doesn't have a skating rink, and wants one built. You go to

your city councilor and pass on this suggestion. Let's also assume that most people in the community think this is a great idea. If there's enough money, the council may vote to approve the building of a skating rink for your community."

But how and when does the rink get built? "From council, the decision goes to the city manager —

City council members attend a lot of meetings. They sit on committees which discuss specific issues such as the budget, parks and recreation, and economic development.

the city employee who handles the day-to-day business of running the city. The manager must figure out how to get the rink built within the budget that we've set." The manager may arrange for land to be purchased and issue a contract to a construction company. Then there is the problem of rerouting traffic during construction. "The details multiply quickly," says Bas. "I know, because the city manager reports back to council on how things are going."

Working together

As a city councilor, Bas has one vote in a council of 15 (14 councilors and the mayor). If he wants to change something, he must persuade a majority of the other councilors to vote with him. "I ran for election to try to correct some things I felt were wrong with the system," says Bas. "Sometimes, I can't do it. Not everyone agrees on the issues. And frankly some people don't want things to change." But just as often, things do work. "I've been able to bring people around. That's the basic part of this career, to be able to represent the views of those who elected me and get things done that matter to them."

Bas uses his newsletter to communicate regularly with his constituents. "People want to know that I'm doing my job," he says, "whether helping to arrange a new recreation hall for students or voting to change an unpopular law."

The recommendations made during committee meetings are also discussed in city council meetings, held in the council chambers shown here.

All in a day's work

Like many elected officials, Bas' days are not predictable. "My schedule depends on who needs me," he laughs. Bas attends the regular council and committee meetings. "There are eight community associations in my area and I sometimes attend their meetings too. At these meetings, I hear about community problems and how people want them solved."

Today, Bas doesn't have any formal council meetings to attend. "If I did," he says, "I'd be too busy to talk to you! Council meetings start at ten in the morning and can go on until midnight."

Complaints and how to deal with them

Dealing with the problems of individual constituents occupies much of Bas's time. "Whenever someone calls with a complaint, I record all the important details. The next step is to find out who to talk to about the complaint." For example, if someone is complaining about speeding cars on their street, Bas contacts the local police and asks them to monitor the speed. If the complaint is about garbage pickup, he calls the supervisor of that department and asks for an explanation.

"After the person I contacted looks into the problem, they call me back and tell me what they can do," says Bas. "I call the person who complained and explain how we're going to solve their problem." When asked if this takes up too much of his time, he shakes his head. "I take the responsibility of representing the people in this community very seriously. When someone has a problem, I want to hear about it."

A constituent is a person who lives in the area represented by a particular elected official. Here, Bas is talking to one of his constituents about an issue of importance to his community. "I wish more people would take the time to come forward and tell me what they think," Bas notes. "It would make my job a lot

It's not all for fun!

You will often find politicians at events ranging from community garage sales to arts festivals. They aren't there just for fun. "We are invited as representatives of the city government," Bas explains. "Our responsibilities may include giving a speech or greeting guests. No matter what, we are expected to represent the city well."

In order to respond as quickly as possible to the numerous telephone calls and messages he receives, Bas has a full-time assistant to help him gather and organize the information he needs.

Homework

Imagine finding out that in two days, you will be tested on the history of your community, local economic trends, and the current state of the electronics industry. That kind of pressure is part of Bas' everyday life. "That information would be the minimum background I'd need to go to a meeting about attracting an electronics company to our city," he says. "How can I talk about issues without the background information? And people expect me to know this community, to understand its traditions as well as its hopes for the future."

How to run for election

When running for election to a public office, you would follow a series of steps. The steps may differ slightly, depending on where you live.
- First, register officially as a candidate with the city clerk. This lets other candidates know you have entered the "race."
- Now you can legally start working on your campaign and raising money to pay for it.
- Next, ask several people who live in the area you want to represent to "nominate" you. These people sign a "nomination document" supporting you as their candidate for elected office. Register this nomination document also.
- During your campaign you may put up signs, distribute brochures, and ask people to vote for you. You may choose to go "door-to-door" to solicit support from voters. You'll also want to find people willing to help with your campaign.

Challenge

Are there any regulations for in-line skating in your community? If you feel strongly about this issue, find out how to appear as a delegation to your city council.

Activity

Debating the issues

One of the issues currently being discussed by some city councilors is the use of in-line skates. Here are two statements about this issue.

Statement A

"I think in-line skates are dangerous. Kids are going to get killed." This councilor believes that the noise from the wheels is loud enough to drown out the sound of approaching cars. Because of this, in-line skates should be banned from all city roads.

Statement B

Another councilor disagreed. She said she had no problem with children skating on dead-end or quiet residential streets, and would not support a city-wide ban. She was also concerned that if the city banned in-line skating, it might start cracking down on other leisure activities, such as street hockey.

Procedure

1. Get a group of friends together. "Elect" one person to be the mayor. The others are councilors.
2. Each person should write down his or her plan for ensuring safe in-line skating in your community. Some points to consider include:
- Should in-line skating be allowed on roads?

- Should it be allowed on sidewalks? Do the skaters pose any danger for pedestrians?
- Could it take place in parks?
- Is in-line skating dangerous for young children?
- What, if any, safety equipment should be mandatory?
- Should rules be made about skating at night or on wet pavement?
3. Hold a council meeting to discuss the issue. The mayor will chair the meeting, but should not take part in the discussion. Each councilor should present his or her plan which must be voted on. If no plan is passed with a majority, the councilors must come up with a compromise. Keep proposing, discussing, and voting until you have a decision on the issue.

How to become a city councilor

Bas got involved with municipal government when he joined a community association. "Taxes were the big issue for us. We found that the tax system had many flaws," says Bas. His community association worked with their city councilor but they weren't happy with the results. "After seeing how city government worked, I felt that I could do a better job," he recalls. "So I decided to run."

In most places, anyone who can vote can run for municipal office. "I started by finding out what I had to do. You need to know about the issues in city politics. You also need to know where you stand on the issues." Bas found this meant making some difficult decisions. "I discovered quickly that there are often good arguments on both sides of an issue," he recalls.

"Once I figured out where I stood on the issues — and filed my intention to run for office with the city clerk — I began working on a campaign strategy." Bas decided to focus on his main strength, his ability to talk to people one-to-one. "I must have knocked on thousands of doors during my campaign," he chuckles. "There's a lot of truth to the saying that politicians need good walking shoes." Bas also had help from friends and people in the area who thought he would do a good job. "That kind of support is essential. You have to have a team that believes in you."

On election day, Bas felt he had a good chance of winning, but he was still very nervous. "I had very mixed feelings watching the results come in," he remembers. "But it turned out well. I won and I've been working as a councilor ever since."

City politics

Constituent: A resident of a politician's community.
By-law: A rule passed by a city council.
Delegation: A group or individual who comes to city council to talk about a particular concern. Sometimes called a **deputation**.
Zoning: A plan for a city that allows certain kinds of development in certain areas, for example, factories can be built in industrial zones, but not in residential zones.

Is this career for you?

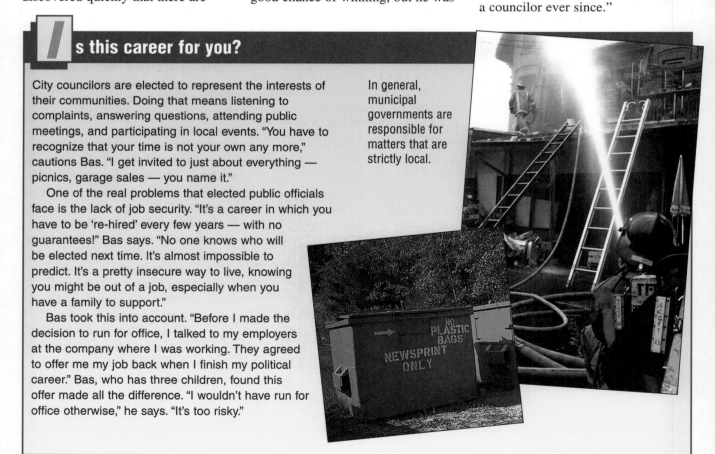

City councilors are elected to represent the interests of their communities. Doing that means listening to complaints, answering questions, attending public meetings, and participating in local events. "You have to recognize that your time is not your own any more," cautions Bas. "I get invited to just about everything — picnics, garage sales — you name it."

One of the real problems that elected public officials face is the lack of job security. "It's a career in which you have to be 're-hired' every few years — with no guarantees!" Bas says. "No one knows who will be elected next time. It's almost impossible to predict. It's a pretty insecure way to live, knowing you might be out of a job, especially when you have a family to support."

Bas took this into account. "Before I made the decision to run for office, I talked to my employers at the company where I was working. They agreed to offer me my job back when I finish my political career." Bas, who has three children, found this offer made all the difference. "I wouldn't have run for office otherwise," he says. "It's too risky."

In general, municipal governments are responsible for matters that are strictly local.

Career planning

"Surf" the Internet for information about the different levels of government. You will be able to find information about responsibilities for each, as well as e-mail addresses for elected officials.

Volunteer to help a local candidate's election campaign. There is plenty of work to be done, and most candidates are more than happy to have students help out.

Making Career Connections

Write to a university or college and request information about political science or public administration courses.

Visit the constituency office of your local councilor or other elected government official. Ask permission to job shadow this person for half a day, taking notes about what the job involves.

Getting started

Interested in being a city councilor? Here's what you can do now.
1. Get involved in student government. If you don't want to run for a position, you can always help out with a campaign.
2. Attend meetings of your local community association or other groups. Learn about the issues of concern to your community and express your own opinions.
3. Keep a file of clippings from the newspaper that concern an issue of interest to you. Write a letter to the editor of the newspaper expressing your views.
4. Study a wide range of topics in high school, including English, politics, history and law.
5. Watch a political debate on television. Pay attention to the rules followed during the debate. Practice your own debating skills by joining a drama, public speaking, or debating club.

Related careers

Here are some related careers you may want to check out.
City or town clerk
Keeps track of all the records in a municipality. Carries out the council's decisions and runs the municipal elections.
Councilor's assistant
Schedules appointments, prepares correspondence, and resolves minor problems for a councilor. Most elected representatives at all levels of government have one or more assistants.
Economic development officer
Responsible for promoting the city in order to attract new businesses and jobs. Usually a non-elected position.
Tax assessor
Visits properties, both business and residential, and estimates their value. Property taxes are based on those estimates.

Future watch

"Certainly there's been an impact from the new communications technology," comments Bas. "My constituents now use e-mail and faxes to express their needs and opinions to me. Anything that helps me keep in touch with people easily and quickly is a great help." While Bas doesn't know his own future plans — "they depend on the next election" — he has little doubt about the task ahead for would-be politicians. "Voters want to elect officials who can balance the needs of the community with the tax dollars available. It's a challenge that must be met."

Don Hale

Police Officer

PERSONAL PROFILE

Career: Police officer. "In this job, I use all my skills and talents. There are rules and regulations, but how I handle a particular situation is ultimately up to me."

Interests: Racquet sports, sailing, and spending time with family. "We live in the country so I also enjoy gardening."

Latest accomplishment: Recently I was on an exam-marking team. These were exams required for promotion from constable to sargeant/detective. It was really interesting working with the others on the team and being involved in the whole process. I learned a lot.

Why I do what I do: "I run into a lot of situations where I can help people and really make a difference. It's not the dramatic kind of stuff you read about in the papers or see on TV, but I get a great deal of satisfaction out of it."

I am: Calm and a good listener. "I take the time to listen to people and really hear what they mean — both fellow officers and the general public. I think we all want to be heard."

What I wanted to be when I was in school: "When I was in high school, I wanted to be a criminal lawyer. Now, I work with lawyers all the time and, no offense intended, but I'm really glad I got into police work instead."

What a police officer does

Police officer Don Hale drives a cruiser for a large city police force. "We're the front line police, the ones the public sees every day," Don explains. "Other officers have other specialties, such as gathering crime-scene evidence to use in court. We even have a few that track computer criminals through cyberspace!"

Don is assigned to a traffic unit responsible for patrolling roads and highways.

Working in hot pursuit

Working in a traffic unit doesn't confine Don simply to stopping speeders. Since most serious crimes involve the use of a car, traffic arrests have always been a way of apprehending criminals as they try to get away. "People who have committed a major felony are sometimes caught just because of the way they are driving," he says.

Whenever Don pulls drivers over for traffic violations, he checks them on the "Mobile Data Terminal." This computer in his cruiser tells Don if the drivers have criminal records or outstanding warrants against them. If there is a warrant for a driver's arrest, or if Don sees something incriminating in the car, he'll approach the driver cautiously. "People who have records or warrants against them have already broken the law. You never know how they will react. They already know they are in trouble when I stop them."

Paperwork and more paperwork

At the end of every shift, officers are required to file complete and accurate reports on their work. "Many people seem to think all police work is exciting. They should try coming off a long, tiring shift and sitting down to write reports!" Don says. "I love my job, but this paperwork isn't fun."

Don also has to keep up with current laws. "Police regulations are constantly changing to reflect the decisions of the government and the courts. It's my responsibility to learn these new rules and regulations. We have to act in a legal manner. If we don't, some of the evidence we collect or present might not be admitted in court and the criminal could get off."

Don uses a computer to file reports on any arrests or other activities that happened during his last shift. "We have to keep accurate records in case they are needed later in court."

All in a day's work

Don's day may begin at different times. "Police officers work a rotating shift. That way, there are police on duty 24 hours a day." The shift Don works — days, evenings, or nights — depends on things such as seniority, who's on vacation, and what's going on in town. "When something special is happening, like the visit of a foreign diplomat or an important government official, we all work extra shifts."

At the start of each shift, Don's unit gets together for a briefing. Assignments are handed out, and any special instructions, bulletins, or memos are read. "Then, we check our equipment," he adds. "After all, our lives could depend on something as simple as having our handcuffs work."

Police officers depend on one another for help in most situations. "I really value the friendships and camaraderie we share," Don says. "Sometimes it's as simple as someone breaking the tension with a good joke."

Now that Don is a sergeant, he is responsible for assigning the officers in his platoon to different duties. During the shift, he supervises from a cruiser, monitoring the radio and assisting with situations as required.

Out on the street

Once the officers hit the streets, they have to rely on their own skills and experience. "There's a great deal of judgment involved," Don explains. "Officers have to decide how to handle each situation, and whether or not to call someone else in."

One incident remains fresh in

Don's mind, even though it happened early in his career. "It was a regular patrol. I started to pull over a car for a traffic violation. But instead of pulling over, the guy took off. I started to follow him but the other vehicle sped up so fast that it left me in the dust."

Because the other car was traveling so fast, Don decided to break off the pursuit. "The faster I drove, the faster he drove to get away from me. I was worried he would hit a pedestrian or another car. I didn't want an innocent bystander to be hurt." Instead, Don called in the license number and make of the car to the dispatcher, along with a description of which way the car was heading. The dispatcher sent other cruisers to intercept it.

"In the old days, we'd get a wagon train effect, with countless cars following a suspect," says Don. "That was really dangerous, because the more cars involved in a pursuit, the more likely one of them will go out of control and hurt someone."

Community policing

Many police officers are actively involved with the community outside of their jobs. Don is no exception. He is a member of *Wing Wheels*, a precision motorcycle team that gives demonstrations at fairs, community events, and schools. "We always get a good response," Don says with a grin. "Maybe it's something about the Harleys. Everyone loves them."

The *Wing Wheels* team does precision riding without dangerous jumps or other stunts. "Our main message is safety," notes Don. *Wing Wheels* also gives the officers the opportunity to meet community members in a non-threatening way. "Some people never meet police officers except when there's trouble," he says. "It helps when they find out we're just regular people too."

A police radio allows officers to keep in touch with the dispatcher at headquarters so they can respond to requests for help.

This story ended tragically. "The car continued driving at an extreme rate of speed, and slammed into a pole," Don recalls. "On impact, the car broke in half and burst into flames. The two passengers were killed but nobody else was hurt." To this day, Don doesn't know for sure why the driver refused to stop.

Dealing with difficult times

In his years as a police officer, Don has dealt with many tragic situations. For him, accident scenes are always

the hardest. "When someone is killed needlessly, there's a pronounced frustration. The worst is when a child is hurt. Everyone involved really suffers." Just recently, he had to deal with a situation where a five-year-old boy was separated from his parents

and wandered into traffic on an expressway. He was struck by an oncoming car and Don didn't think he would live. "We were really fearful for him," says Don, "but as it turns out, he is well on his way to a full recovery, and ought to be able to lead a normal life. Sometimes you get lucky."

No matter how bad a situation is, the officers involved still have to do their jobs. Later they can deal with their own emotions. "We usually discuss it among ourselves afterward," says Don. "We're close enough that we can express our emotions and we watch each other for signs of distress."

Activity

Deciphering fingerprints

When officers fingerprint a suspect, they first roll each finger on an ink pad, and then roll each finger from one side to the other on a page which has a box for each finger. Even though it is called "fingerprinting," Don says they actually do more than that. "Once we have the suspect's fingerprints, we also print both the right and left palms on the same piece of paper. It gives us more identifying features."

You will need
- a stamp pad with washable ink
- blank pieces of paper

Procedure
1. Get together with three or four friends and make complete sets of all your fingerprints. Make sure to identify the prints with the person's name and finger description (right hand middle finger, etc.).

2. Ask each person to take three new pieces of paper and print a single fingerprint (any finger) on each page. Police officers rarely have whole prints to use for matching, so make at least one of these prints just part of a finger. Write your name and the finger name on the back of each sheet. These are the "mystery" prints.
3. Mix up the mystery prints and number them on the front. Now, try to match each "mystery" print with one from the named sets. You'll soon discover that it's much more difficult than it seems!

Challenge

Work with the same people that did this activity with you. Each person should handle a clean drinking glass, marking it secretly with a wax pencil or sticker on the bottom. Find any fingerprints on each glass by sprinkling the glass with talcum powder. Stick a piece of clear tape on any fingerprints you find to protect them from smudging. Now, who handled each glass?

As a routine, every person charged with a serious criminal offense is fingerprinted and photographed. Their fingerprints are filed and can be used as a reference in the future. Reading fingerprints is not easy, and requires special training. You can try deciphering them yourself in this activity.

How to become a police officer

Don's mother first spotted the newspaper ad for the local police department. "I was sceptical. I didn't think it was for me," admits Don. "But my mother talked me into it. She knew that I was interested in law, but I wasn't exactly sure what I wanted to do. She thought it would be a good job to have while I made up my mind. Also, a relative was a police officer and my mom thought I was a similar kind of person. I guess she was right, because I love police work."

After Don applied for the job, he had to wait for a response. When a letter arrived from the police department, he was too nervous to open it. "I had that letter for two days before a friend took it upon himself to open it." He laughs "That's when I found out I got in."

Don reported to the police college for weeks of study and physical training. Recruits study law and police regulations and procedures. Physical training and self-defense classes take up a lot of time, too. When they finish in the classroom, recruits are sent out with an experienced officer who takes them along on investigations and evaluates their performance. "The training was tough," recalls Don. "There was so much to learn." He grins. "And I had a really strict instructor."

Successful recruits are sworn in as police officers. "That was a very important moment in my life," Don nods. "It was the first time that my relatives saw me in uniform. I couldn't believe how proud I felt."

Traffic signals

When a really bad accident occurs, an officer may need to change the traffic lights. In the past, when this happened, an officer would open the "traffic box," which was located on one of the street corners, and manually change the pattern of the lights. Today, the traffic signals in most large cities are computerized. "I call the dispatcher who calls the computer center," says Don. "They change the lights to flash red or yellow, while I direct traffic."

Is this career for you?

Don says one of the most important assets for a police officer is the ability to stay calm. "There are situations — accidents or physical contact — when I can't afford to get worked up," says Don. "I have to maintain control. That's why people call the police. They need someone who can calmly take charge."

Officers also have to develop a "thick skin." "I see a lot of pain and suffering. I've become hardened to it to a certain extent, but it's still really tough." He also recommends you have a lot of patience. "People often try to vent their anger on me," says Don. "Like when I pull someone over for speeding. They're angry but they're really angry at themselves. I get tired of it but I don't let it get to me."

Don feels that his family benefits from his career. Police officers receive good benefits, such as job security and flexibility. Because officers sometimes work extra shifts, they can accumulate days off. "I have time to spend with my family and to get involved in community activities," he says.

People expect police officers to be calm, patient, and knowledgeable — good people to talk to.

The bottom line? "I'd recommend this career," Don states firmly. "I put a lot into what I do. And I help people. Together, that means I'm pretty satisfied at the end of the day."

Career planning

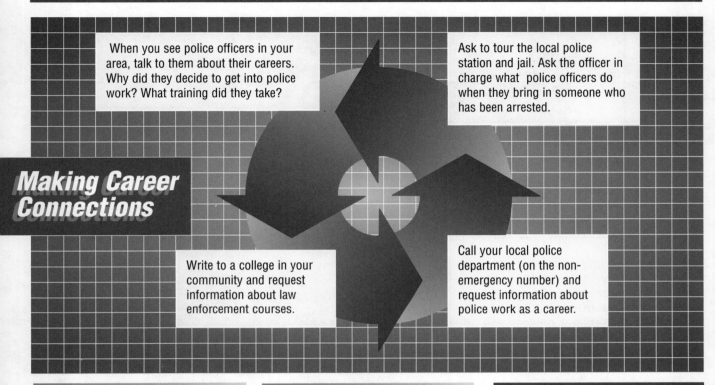

When you see police officers in your area, talk to them about their careers. Why did they decide to get into police work? What training did they take?

Ask to tour the local police station and jail. Ask the officer in charge what police officers do when they bring in someone who has been arrested.

Making Career Connections

Write to a college in your community and request information about law enforcement courses.

Call your local police department (on the non-emergency number) and request information about police work as a career.

Getting started

Interested in being a police officer? Here's what you can do now.

1. Read newspaper stories involving legal cases. Imagine what roles the police played in each case.
2. Stay in good physical shape. Go to your local police department and ask about the physical requirements to join their force. Ask what exercises you could do to stay fit.
3. Develop your powers of observation. Observe a room for about 10-20 seconds. Then leave, and write down as many details as possible about the room. It's not as easy as it sounds but you'll get better with practice.
4. Become a volunteer at a hospital. Learn to listen objectively to other people's stories.
5. Study a wide range of topics in high school, including math, computer sciences, English, history, and law.

Related careers

Here are some related careers you may want to check out.

Security guard
Guards a particular place or person. In malls, may be disguised as a regular shopper to help catch shoplifters.

Prosecutor
A lawyer who works to convict suspects. Works with the police as a team, gathering evidence and preparing a case.

911 Operator
Answers emergency calls and dispatches police officers, ambulances, and/or fire fighters. Must remain calm and figure out what services are needed for each emergency.

Private investigator
Gathers evidence for cases. Often handles cases where no illegal activity has occurred, such as finding a missing relative.

Future watch

Now that many businesses rely on computers, computer-assisted fraud has increased. This has led to a growing need for police officers with strong computer skills. Police forces are also using computers to help solve crimes. Instruments such as the Mobile Data Terminal give officers immediate access to data while on patrol. Many police departments also have computer access to other police organizations around the world, such as Interpol in Europe. These organizations and their databases are making it easier to get information and solve crimes.

Law Librarian

PERSONAL PROFILE

Career: Law librarian. "It's detective work. I search for whatever information lawyers need for their cases — no matter how unusual."

Interests: Reading, camping, sports. "I love to read! As a kid, I was a big bookworm."

Latest accomplishment: "I've just been promoted; my new title is Coordinator of Information Services."

Why I do what I do: "Every case is different. I don't get bored because I never know what I might be involved in next. I also get to meet some really interesting people."

I am: Inquisitive. "In this job it helps to be nosy!"

What I wanted to be when I was in school: "I wasn't sure. I took a law course in high school but I didn't think I wanted to be a lawyer. I was interested in history, then couldn't decide what to do with it."

What a law librarian does

Law librarians such as Esther Wan do what most librarians do — work with information. A law librarian specializes in information that applies to the legal system. "Lawyers depend on me to find information they need for their cases."

Esther Wan works for a law library in a large university. "When a lawyer comes in looking for some detail or point of law, I help them use the library's resources." She also trains law students. "I show them how to use many of the same research tools I use," she explains. "They learn how to access information using law book guides, printed and electronic indexes, and computer databases.

Is there a precedent?

"Most of the time, lawyers who come to the library are looking for 'statutes' and 'precedents,'" Esther says. A statute is a law exactly as the government wrote it. A precedent is any decision made in the past on a similar case. "Statutes are important, because lawyers want to read the exact wording of any laws that might apply to their cases." She grins. "But no matter how precise the wording, laws can often be interpreted in more than one way. That's why precedents are also necessary."

For example, imagine a law that states that a person must wear a helmet while riding a bicycle on a road. "That's the statute," explains Esther. "However, a judge might rule that 'road' also means sidewalks. This would be a precedent.

"Often, unusual cases or those involving new technology don't have precedents," comments Esther. "Bioengineering, computer fraud, theft over the Internet — these are so new, our courts may not have dealt with these issues before."

A lawyer working on an unusual case might ask Esther to look for precedents in other countries. "Our library keeps law books containing statutes and cases from the United States, Canada, and the United Kingdom. All three have similar legal systems, and I often find useful details in their law books."

You want to know what?

Law librarians also look for other types of information. Sometimes the questions aren't easy and Esther may spend hours trying to find an answer. "One lawyer asked me to find the vacancy rate for downtown offices," she recalls. "I didn't know where to start looking for that! One of my colleagues was asked to find out how much beer weighs." Esther sighs. "Some requests seem downright silly, but the information may be very important to a case."

Much of Esther's day is spent checking through stacks of law books that describe past cases.

When working with law students, Esther's role is different from when she works with lawyers. "I don't usually find the answers for them," she says. "I teach them how to find their own."

All in a day's work

Esther's day begins when the library opens in the morning. "Our hours are posted, so people know when they can come in for information." Today, she starts by working at the reference desk. "There is always someone here," she says, "so anyone with a question can find help.

"Most of my time at the reference desk I'm talking to people," Esther says. "All kinds of people come in with all sorts of requests. It keeps me on my toes!" Each request is for very specific information. "Lawyers are experienced in using the library resources, so they know exactly what to ask for. They also expect me to find it very quickly."

Small claims court

One visitor is someone who wouldn't usually visit a law library. "This person is presenting a case in small claims court," Esther says.

There are no lawyers in small claims court. The people involved tell their stories directly to the judge, who then makes a decision. "The judge realizes that these people don't know as much about the law as a lawyer, but still expects them to have done their research."

This may mean going to the law library for information. "I have to be very careful when I help someone in this situation," comments Esther. "I'm not qualified to give legal advice, although I sometimes get asked. I concentrate on helping people find the appropriate information. But I can't tell them what it means or how to use it in court."

The search begins

After lunch, Esther leaves the reference desk and concentrates on tracking down information. "Some users leave their requests with me. I find the information as quickly as I can, but sometimes it takes several days." She spends a lot of time on the computer databases searching for information electronically.

"The computer revolution has changed the way law libraries work," she states. "A lot of what we used to get from printed materials is now on databases and CD-ROMs. It makes our job both easier and more difficult. It's easier because the computer does a lot of the time-

Moot court

As part of their training, senior law students participate in mock trials known as moots. "Moots are conducted like real trials, and the students have to prepare the cases as if they were really going to court. It gets pretty crazy around here when they are all trying to find information at the same time," laughs Esther.

Even in the 1800s, mock trials were used to help train law students. These students, in 1897, were able to use a real court room for their moot. One of their professors acted as the judge.

consuming detail work, such as going through indexes. The difficult part is knowing how to use all this technology." While new graduates in library technology have learned about computers, many other librarians learned on the job. "We all have to study to keep up with new computer technology and new software.

"Sometimes I wonder about the people whose lives are discussed in these books. Did they ever think that what happened to them would echo into the future?"

Lawyer Rob Pattison (see page 42) often looks up information in the library Esther works in. Here, he does some quick research before going into court. In some countries, lawyers wear "robes" in court.

A new crowd

Just when Esther's day is winding down, a large group of students pours into the library. She gets ready to help them. "I enjoy the teaching aspect of my job," she says. "The students are great. They do want to learn, but they sometimes try to get me to do a bit extra for them. As long as they come out of here knowing what they need, I don't really mind."

(see page 42)

Activity

Digging up details

Among the people Esther helps are those appearing in small claims court. These people have no legal training, but must present a well-researched argument to a judge. Try this for yourself in this activity!

You will need
access to a library and/or computer on-line to the Internet

Procedure
1. Choose one of the following scenarios as your reason for being in "small claims court."
   - Your dog bit a delivery person who wants compensation for medical expenses and lost wages.
   - You worked at a fast food restaurant for the summer, and you didn't receive your last pay check. The manager says you did.
   - The library says you have ten overdue library books. The fine is more than the cost of the books. You want to convince the judge to reduce the fine.
   - You planted a tree at the edge of your property and cared for it over the years. One day, the person next door cut the tree down, claiming that it blocked the sun. You want this person to replace the tree.
2. Make a list of any facts or information you could use to convince the judge of the value of your case. For example, if you were defending yourself from the delivery person's claim, you would look up the local laws on dog ownership.
3. Research your information. Use any library resources that would help you, including the Internet, if available.
4. Prepare your case. Plan the order in which you would present each relevant piece of information to the judge. Sum up your information in a closing statement. Test how convincing you are by arguing your case with a friend.

Challenge

Choose a local issue that interests or affects you. Follow the steps in this activity to prepare a "brief," a written argument that presents information and gives your point of view. Send your brief to the group or politician involved with this issue.

I KNOW IT'S IN HERE SOMEWHERE.

Is this person likely to convince the judge of his arguments? Why?

How to become a law librarian

Law librarians come from many backgrounds but they all have one thing in common: training in information technology. "It wasn't necessary in the past," Esther says, "but now there are so many skills to learn that it would be difficult to get a job in this specialty without that training."

Although Esther belonged to the library club in high school, she didn't think of it as a career until much later. "Like everyone else, I considered lots of careers and couldn't settle on one." She studied a wide range of subjects, including math, law, history, and English. "Then I went on to earn a bachelor's degree in history."

By this point, Esther had decided on a career in library science. "I enrolled in a master's program in library science. The main

requirement was a degree in another subject area. That makes sense," she says. "All fields — science, liberal arts, fine arts — have specialized libraries and need librarians who understand the subjects."

Focusing on the law

While in the library science program, Esther studied a range of subjects, including computer science and statistics. "We were also trained to assist people," she says. "This is a very service-oriented business." She decided to specialize in law. "During my first summer, I worked for a law firm library. That convinced me."

Esther's first two jobs were with large law firms. "Long hours and a hectic pace, but exciting!" she recalls. The switch to the law library was a personal choice. "I really like working with people, helping and teaching. I know I made the right decision."

In the past, law librarians used books, journals, newspapers, and other printed materials. Now, modern technology is rapidly changing the law library. "We use computers to access information stored on CD-ROMs," says Esther. "Legal databases are also available through the Internet."

Is this career for you?

"Some people have the idea that librarians are shy, quiet people who keep their noses in books all day," says Esther. "Nothing could be further from the truth. In this job I have to deal with the public. If you don't enjoy talking to people, this is not the job for you."

Esther says a good librarian has to have more than a friendly personality. "Good librarians have to be able to find things. If they can't find the information directly, they should be able to send the person to someone else who can help them."

It also means not giving up. "Sometimes a piece of information takes hours to locate, and may be buried under a pile of other things. You can't get frustrated and stop trying."

While Esther enjoys her job, she admits there is a down side. "Law is a very high-pressure field. There are a lot of people under stress." She smiles. "I try to keep calm. And it helps to have a sense of humor."

Career planning

Making Career Connections

Call a large law firm and ask permission to "job shadow" a law librarian. Follow the person for half a day, taking notes about what the job involves.

Talk to your school librarians. Ask how they got into the field, and what they find most interesting about their jobs. Ask how you can access library catalogs through the Internet.

Write to a university or college and request information about information technology (library science) courses.

Call a law library and request a tour. Ask for a demonstration of how they use their computer system to access information.

Getting started

Interested in becoming a law librarian? Here's what you can do now.

1. Offer to help in the school or public library, or join the library club if there is one.
2. Read newspaper stories involving legal cases. What kinds of information might the lawyers need?
3. When doing research, go to the school or public library. Try new sources of information to practice using the resources.
4. Learn to access information using a computer, and explore the on-line resources of the Internet.
5. Organize your books and magazines so that any information they contain is easy to find.
6. Invite a law librarian, lawyer, or law clerk to speak to your class about careers in law.
7. Study a wide range of topics in high school, including math, computer sciences, English, history, and law.

Related careers

Here are some related careers you may want to check out.

Public librarian
Works in a public library. Provides information to visitors, maintains the collection, and may also develop and organize electronic files.

Court reporter
Records everything that is said in court during a trial. Prepares transcripts of each day's proceedings.

Television researcher
Obtains background information for news stories from libraries, newspapers, etc. Helps reporters provide complete coverage of a news story.

Legal editor
Copy edits and proofreads law books to make sure the information is accurate and the grammar and spelling are correct. May work on "hard copy" (a manuscript on paper) or on-screen.

Future watch

"Some experts predict that in 20 years, law books won't be printed any more," Esther says. "The information will be stored electronically on computer files!" That's not to say that books will disappear. "They are still easier for most people to use." But libraries themselves may change. "Many libraries are now on-line," she notes. "People at home or at work can use their computers to obtain information from the library. The librarian's role will be to maintain the electronic database and ensure that the information is up-to-date and relevant."

Jeff Kendall

School Board Trustee

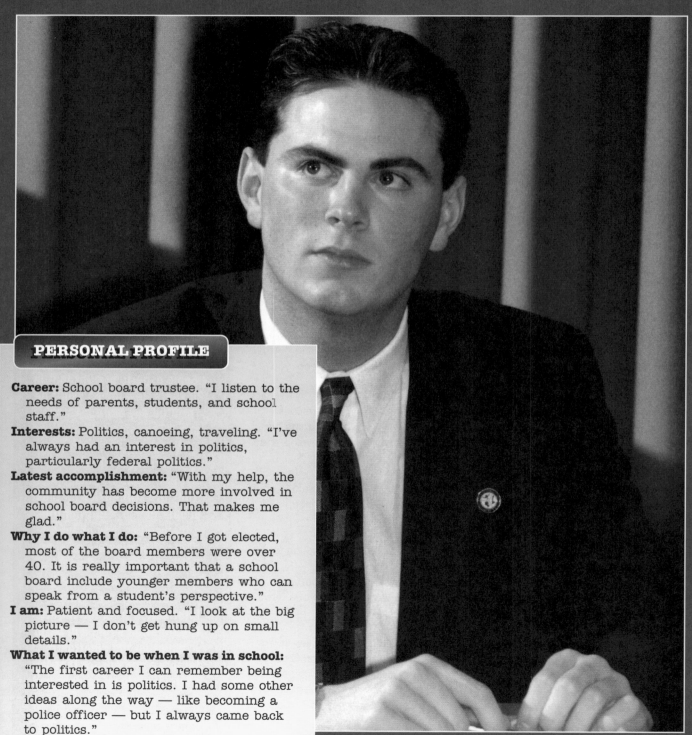

PERSONAL PROFILE

Career: School board trustee. "I listen to the needs of parents, students, and school staff."

Interests: Politics, canoeing, traveling. "I've always had an interest in politics, particularly federal politics."

Latest accomplishment: "With my help, the community has become more involved in school board decisions. That makes me glad."

Why I do what I do: "Before I got elected, most of the board members were over 40. It is really important that a school board include younger members who can speak from a student's perspective."

I am: Patient and focused. "I look at the big picture — I don't get hung up on small details."

What I wanted to be when I was in school: "The first career I can remember being interested in is politics. I had some other ideas along the way — like becoming a police officer — but I always came back to politics."

What a school board trustee does

Many students think that their principal makes up all the rules. In reality, many school rules are based on the policies set by the school board. Jeff Kendall is a trustee—a member of a school board. "Today's public school system began mainly as community efforts," Jeff explains. "Community members were elected to help provide a school for local children. These groups were the first school boards.

"Today's school boards are still elected by the community," says Jeff. "The number of schools may vary, but a board may look after as many as several hundred schools."

Money for schools

"Taxes are collected from community members, and some of this money goes to the school board," Jeff says. The board decides how and where money should be spent. "If your school needed a new gymnasium, your prinicpal would make a request to the board. That request would be added to those from all the other schools." The members of the board meet and discuss the requests. "There is only so much money to go around, so some requests have to wait until next year. We try to give every school what they need, but we want to make sure money is well spent."

Many people in government, like Jeff and Bas Balkissoon (page 10), are elected to office by their community members. These women are about to vote in the election.

Making school policy

A major responsibility of the school board is to set policy. Setting policy means deciding on rules that will apply to all the schools. This can take a great deal of discussion and research before the board reaches a decision. "My board had to set a policy on expulsion recently. We were concerned about the amount of violence in the schools. Some school staff came to the board and suggested a policy of expelling students who carry a weapon at school. Board members thought it was a good idea."

But not everyone was happy with the proposed policy. "At the next board meeting, some students came to say that the policy was too harsh," Jeff recalls. "Other students showed up to support it. We heard all the opinions and then voted. The vote passed the new policy. That means it's the rule now."

Community concerns

Jeff also represents the school board to the community that elected him. "I'm often asked to speak about educational issues," he says. "These issues have changed over the years." Once, the main concern was literacy — making sure everyone learned to read and write. "Literacy and numeracy are still the core," Jeff adds, "but today's boards have to face new issues such as changing technology. A few years ago, computers were a novelty. Today, schools are hurrying to hook up to the Internet and communicate internationally. It's hard for decision-makers to keep up."

Where does a typical school board spend most of its money? Does any area receive more funds than you expected? Why might this be so?

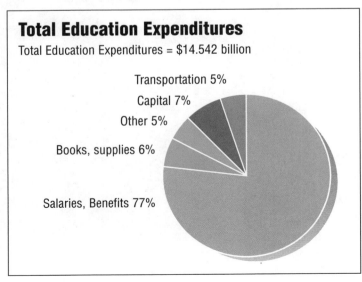

Total Education Expenditures

Total Education Expenditures = $14.542 billion

Transportation 5%
Capital 7%
Other 5%
Books, supplies 6%
Salaries, Benefits 77%

All in a day's work

Jeff's position is considered a part-time job so he doesn't keep regular office hours. He juggles his board responsibilities with his own college schedule. "I'm studying politics, but with all my school board work, I don't carry a full class load."

On most days, Jeff starts by going through his mail. "Dealing with correspondence is a big part of this job," he says. "Every letter has to be answered and that can be very time-consuming." He also returns phone calls and schedules appointments such as speaking engagements or meetings with staff members. To do his job properly, he has to stay in touch with the board officials as well as the staff in the schools in his area. "I find a good time to meet with them is over the lunch hour."

So many meetings

"Meetings take most of my time," Jeff notes. "And most of them are at night." Evening meetings make it possible for parents to voice their concerns. "My schedule fills up quickly," he adds. "I try to meet regularly with the parent-teacher association of each school. That way I find out what's going on in the community. If parents want better science equipment or more time for music teaching, that's where I hear about it. Then I

Up-to-date technology is expensive, but the benefits are great.

Who's to blame for all that homework?

Do your teachers give you homework to do every night? Maybe you shouldn't be blaming them for it. Many school boards have a written policy stating how much homework to give students. At Jeff's board, the guidelines for homework are as follows:

Grades 1-3: up to 20 minutes, occasionally.

Grades 4-6: up to 45 minutes, two or three times per week.

Grades 7-9: up to 60 minutes daily.

Grades 10 and up: beyond 60 minutes daily, to include assignments and review.

What is your board's policy about homework?

Jeff often performs ceremonial duties, such as presenting awards at graduations or making speeches at official functions. At age 20, he is one of the youngest school board trustees in his board's history. "My age is a real asset when I make decisions," he comments.

talk about their concerns at the next board meeting."

Board meetings take place once a month. "Then we have committee meetings at least once a week." Jeff shrugs. "I knew about the hours before I ran for election — I'm getting used to it.

"It's really important to be prepared before I go into a meeting," says Jeff. "I find out as much as I can about each item on the meeting's agenda. Meetings can be very, very long if trustees ask questions that they should have investigated beforehand."

Say what?

Politics, like any human activity, has its own "jargon," or specialized words. Here are a few.

Quorum: The minimum number of people who must be present at a meeting before they can vote on something. Two-thirds of the membership is a common quorum.

Delegation: People who appear before the board or any organization to make their views known. A delegation usually represents a larger group.

Minutes: The official record of what goes on at a meeting. Minutes from the previous meeting are read to check that they are accurate. Once this is done, the minutes are accepted and become a legal record.

Survey

I am asking members of my family for their opinions about our coming holiday plans. The results of this survey will help us decide where to spend our vacation.

1. Circle the number that best describes your feelings about each of these ideas. (1 is "don't like it" and 5 is "great idea.")

   (a) visiting grandparents' farm   1 2 3 4 5
   (b) renting a cottage   1 2 3 4 5
   (c) going wilderness camping   1 2 3 4 5
   (d) visiting friends in New York   1 2 3 4 5
   (e) staying home   1 2 3 4 5

2. How important is it to you that the family spends its vacation together? (1 is "not important," and 5 is "very important.")   1 2 3 4 5

Activity

Who cares?

Jeff Kendall spends a lot of time finding out what matters to people. "Some people come right up and tell me their concerns," he notes, "but other people prefer to answer questions on a survey." You can use a survey of your own to find out who cares about certain issues in your classroom or family.

You will need
- a clipboard
- survey forms (prepared in this activity)

Procedure
1. Prepare your survey form. You could do a general survey to find out what your fellow students or family think. Or, if you are aware of an issue that matters, write your survey questions about that issue. Be sure to include the following information.
   - State the purpose of your survey.
   - Explain what you will do with your results.

- You may also wish to add: *"Please do not put your name on this page."* If possible, use a word processor or typewriter to produce the final copy.
2. Make sure you have permission from your teacher or family to conduct your survey.
3. Photocopy your survey form and distribute it. Allow people time to complete it.
4. Collect the completed survey forms. Analyze them and list the results in a table. Include the

Use this sample survey form to help you with your own.

number of surveys distributed and the number filled out.
5. Assess your results. Were they what you expected? Why or why not? How useful is a survey in finding out public opinion?
6. Do what you said you would do with your results, even if you don't agree with them.

How to become a school board trustee

"**G**et elected!" says Jeff. "Any citizen can run for the school board provided they are of the legal age to vote. There aren't any formal education requirements."

Before you consider a career as a school board trustee, Jeff recommends you find out if the trustees in your area work part-time or full-time. "But even being a part-time member takes up an amazing amount of time," he cautions. "You have to be prepared for that."

Running for office

To become a trustee, you must successfully "run for office" in an election. Sometimes there's a lot of competition. When Jeff ran for his position, there were five other candidates. "To be successful, you have to know the issues," he says. "I focused my campaign on spending money wisely and on improving educational programs. I thought those were the most important issues — and the voters agreed with me!"

During his election campaign, Jeff attended all-candidates meetings, delivered brochures to the homes in his area, put up signs, and talked to voters. "Running a campaign is tough work," he recalls. "I spent hours talking to people about the issues. It was all very stressful because I didn't know how it was going to turn out."

The time commitment and the stress didn't go away after Jeff won the election. "I found that out right away," he laughs. "I must still keep up with the issues. My reading pile is huge!" He also writes a newsletter to explain the issues to his community. "Sometimes I run out of day before I run out of work."

Is this career for you?

Any elected official must truly enjoy working with people. It also helps to be able to communicate well. "In this job I deal with the public every day," says Jeff. "I need to listen and understand, and then convey their concerns to others."

While Jeff must listen to everyone, he can't forget that he represents all the residents of his school district. "I have to do what's best for the whole community. I can't let my personal feelings or the interests of just a few people cloud my judgment."

Dealing with problems

A difficult part of Jeff's job is dealing with reporters. They often attend board meetings and talk to board members. "I'm careful about what I say to reporters — and how I say it," Jeff says. "I try to make sure that there are no misunderstandings printed in the newspaper."

Another difficult part is dealing with unhappy parents or students. "I can understand how they feel," he says. "It matters to parents what their kids are being taught and how the schools are being run. It's my role to listen and deal with whatever problems exist."

Television is a useful way of communicating with the public. On this local TV program, Jeff was in a panel debate. "It gave me a chance to express the views of my community."

Career planning

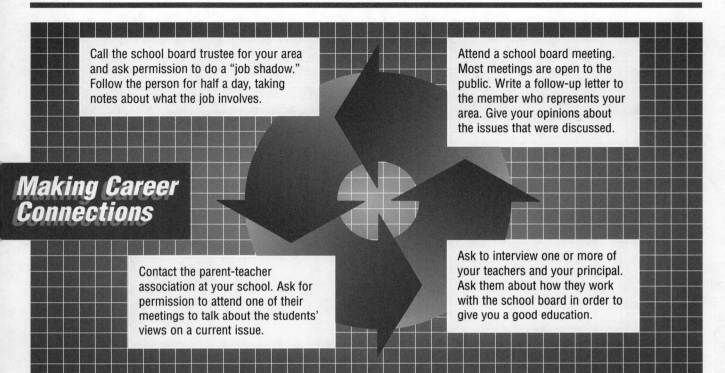

Call the school board trustee for your area and ask permission to do a "job shadow." Follow the person for half a day, taking notes about what the job involves.

Attend a school board meeting. Most meetings are open to the public. Write a follow-up letter to the member who represents your area. Give your opinions about the issues that were discussed.

Making Career Connections

Contact the parent-teacher association at your school. Ask for permission to attend one of their meetings to talk about the students' views on a current issue.

Ask to interview one or more of your teachers and your principal. Ask them about how they work with the school board in order to give you a good education.

Getting started

Interested in being a school board trustee? Here's what you can do now.
1. Join a club at school. Run for election as treasurer, because treasurers are responsible for budget planning.
2. Get involved in student government. Run for office, or help on a friend's campaign.
3. Most schools or school boards have a policy on the rights and responsibilities of students. Obtain a copy of the policy that applies to you. Think about why these rules were put in place.
4. Join the debating club at school. You can debate matters of school policy, and invite a member of your school board to take part in one of your debates.
5. Everything you study in high school would be good background for a school board member.

Related careers

Here are some related careers you may want to check out.
Teacher
Delivers the curriculum in one or more subject areas or grades. Follows policies and decisions made by the board.
School secretary
Carries out the administration functions in a school. Organizes and maintains student records, school schedules, and other important data.
Educational writer
Writes documents required by school boards outlining policy or regulations. May also work as journalists, reporting on educational issues, or produce textbooks.
Superintendent
A non-elected position on the school board. Ensures that schools follow the policies of the school board. Provides advice to the elected board members.

Future watch

With so many exciting changes happening in technology and communications, the role of school board trustees is even more important. "There are hard choices ahead about the cost of new technologies, and how the technology can be best used for education," Jeff says. "I think voters will elect individuals who show that they understand technology — and money management." Board trustees must also be more flexible than in the past. "There are profound changes in education occurring everywhere," he adds. "We need public officials who are willing to listen to new ideas."

Lisa Stadelbauer

Foreign Service Officer

PERSONAL PROFILE

Career: Foreign service officer. "I represent my country's interests in other countries."

Interests: Reading, golf, and travel. "I love to travel. Because my work lets me live in different places, I learn so much more than if I were just visiting."

Latest accomplishment: "I was in the Middle East when a great deal of progress was being made towards peace. It was a very exciting time."

Why I do what I do: "Traveling to other countries was the big attraction for me. I've already done and seen more things than I ever thought I would."

I am: Interested in other cultures. "I'm not very outgoing, but I try."

What I wanted to be when I was in school: "I had no idea. I went through stages — teacher, lawyer, and writer."

What a foreign service officer does

Foreign service officers like Lisa Stadelbauer work for the federal government. They represent their country in other countries around the world. "Part of the job is to help with the business and personal arrangements of our citizens and theirs," Lisa says.

Lisa's office is located inside the "embassy," her government's official building in the host country. "The senior government official at the embassy is called the ambassador."

Where in the world?

Members of the foreign service have some choice in where they will work. "Assignments abroad are called

Adapting to a foreign language and foreign customs is one of the most difficult parts of living in another country. Foreign officers often have training in several languages. "I wanted a picture of this sign," Lisa recalls. "It was fun."

postings," explains Lisa. "We request where we'd like to go and the government tries to accommodate requests. But we don't always get our first choice." Postings last from two to five years. Lisa was pleased with her first posting. "I went to Tel Aviv, Israel."

Serving your country

The duties of a foreign service officer depend on where the embassy is located and what tasks need to be done. For example, on Lisa's assignment to Israel, she worked in the "consular" program. "I did a variety of things," she recalls. "We helped tourists from our home country who had medical emergencies or problems such as lost or stolen passports or wallets. We also provided information about our country to interested Israelis."

She also helps those who want to immigrate. "People wanting to come

and live in our country usually apply to our embassy first," Lisa explains. "We help them with the paperwork and make sure they know the entrance requirements."

International trade

Assisting individuals is only part of the foreign service officer's role. "Trade is very important," Lisa agrees. "These days, business is becoming more and more international. So we gave advice to companies in my country that wanted to market their goods in Israel." Everyone working in an embassy learns some of the laws and customs of the host country. "We can explain any customs that are different from those we have at home."

The embassy staff also knows how business is usually conducted in other countries. "Running a meeting in Vancouver or New York can be different from running one in other places," she notes. In Japan, for example, custom dictates who may speak first. "Our knowledge of the host country helps businesses avoid costly or embarrassing mistakes, and helps promote trade at the same time."

Diplomatic Service officers help Canadian business people who may wish to expand into a new market.

All in a day's work

Lisa says there is no routine in the foreign service. "You never know what the day might have in store for you," she says. "It's always a surprise." Although she usually works business hours — 9:00 a.m. to 5:00 p.m. — emergencies rarely follow a schedule. "We all take a turn working evenings and weekends as well as weekdays," she explains. "Someone is on call at the embassy 24 hours a day, every day."

Go to jail

When Lisa was in Israel, she assisted tourists who ran into difficulty, including those who had been arrested for various crimes. "People have the idea that the embassy can get them out of jail. That simply isn't true," she says. "People who break the law while in a foreign country are prosecuted just like anyone else. What we can do is find them a lawyer, notify their families back home, and make sure they're treated fairly under the laws of that country."

Lisa also deals with some strange requests. "There's always someone who feels it's the embassy's duty to send them back home when they run out of money." One man reported a stolen wallet, and wanted airfare home. "When I talked to him, it turned out he didn't have enough money to get home even before his wallet was taken! I suggested he sell some of his possessions to raise the money instead."

The final journey

Lisa sometimes has the sad task of contacting the family of someone who has died. "It's never an easy thing to do," she admits. "I'll never forget the man who died while on

Gestures around the world

Smiles and frowns mean the same wherever you live, but what about nodding your head? The meanings of such gestures depend on local customs. Compare these examples to your own customs.

- In Taiwan, it is impolite to blink your eyes at another person.
- In Australia, it is improper to wink at a woman, even to express friendship.
- In Holland, a circular motion of the finger around the ear means someone has a phone call.
- In Bulgaria and Greece, nodding your head up and down means "no."
- In Paraguay, crossing two fingers is an offensive gesture.
- In Finland, folding your arms across your chest is a sign of arrogance and pride.
- In Fiji, folded arms show disrespect.

Driving around the world

If you want to drive a car in another country, get an International Driving Permit (IDP) before leaving home. An IDP is not needed in all countries — for instance, Canadians can drive in the United States and vice versa with a current driver's license. However, in most parts of the world — from Afghanistan to Zimbabwe — an IDP is required.

In most countries, cars are driven on the right side of the road. There are a few exceptions — Great Britain, Australia, and Japan, for example — where drivers drive on the left side. That can take getting used to, especially when turning corners and backing onto the street!

vacation here. His family wanted him to be buried in Israel but couldn't afford to attend the funeral themselves. I looked after all the arrangements for them." Lisa pauses. "And I went to the service. It seemed the least I could do."

Home

Following Lisa's two-year posting in Israel, she was assigned to an office at home. "I experienced a bit of culture shock coming back," she says, "and it surprised me. You expect to take time getting used to a different country. You don't expect that when you come home."

Lisa visited Akko, Israel, on a day off. "One of the benefits of this job is getting to see unusual parts of the world."

Challenge

Use an atlas to locate each of the countries and cities mentioned in this activity. Choose one city and imagine you are being posted there as a foreign service officer. Research the culture and traditions of the area. Make a list of other information that could help you "settle in." (Hint: contact that country's embassy in your country, using the Internet.)

Activity

They speak Guarani, don't they?

Foreign service officers must learn all they can about different countries. Geography is a good place to start. Test your own geographic knowledge by doing the following quiz.

Procedure

1. Copy the list of countries. Beside each, write where the country is located: Asia, Europe, North America, Central America, South America, Australasia, Africa, or the Middle East.
2. Match each country with its capital city.
3. Match each country with its major spoken language(s).

4. After completing the quiz, use the answers on page 48 to rate your geographic knowledge. Which parts of the world did you know most about? Which parts do you need to learn more about?

How do you rate?

Country	Capital Cities	Spoken Language(s)
Afghanistan	Andorra la Vella	Catalan, French, Castilian
Andorra	Asunción	English, Maori
Austria	Brussels	Flemish, French, German
Belgium	Cayenne	French, Creole
French Guiana	Guatemala	French
Guadeloupe	Kabul	German
Malta	Valletta	Maltese, English
New Zealand	Vienna	Pashtu, Persian, Turkic
Paraguay	Wellington	Spanish, Guarani

How to become a foreign service officer

Lisa didn't hear about the foreign service until she completed a degree in commerce. "A friend of mine told me he was going to write the foreign service exam," she explains. "My first response was 'What's the foreign service?' When I looked into it, I realized this was the career for me.

"I was warned it was a really tough field to get into," Lisa recalls. The first hurdle was the foreign service exam. Fortunately, she had taken the right courses in high school. "I took a little bit of everything, including French and history," she says. "I also liked reading the newspaper. So I had a good general knowledge of the world and of current and historical events." This knowledge helped her pass the exam.

"Knowing more than one language is a big help," Lisa suggests. Other qualifications change from time to time, but a college degree is necessary. "Good choices are business, commerce, political science, or public policy."

Once she passed the written exam, Lisa went to several interviews. In one interview, "I had to imagine that a student from my country was traveling abroad and was caught with illegal drugs," she recalls. "The interviewers wanted to hear what I would tell the student's parents." Lisa nods. "At the time, I wondered how real that situation was. Now I know. That sort of thing can happen every day. Part of this career is dealing with people in trouble far from home."

She smiles. "And the rest is about experiencing the world."

Is this career for you?

"Choosing the foreign service as a career is a family choice. Everyone you care about is affected," explains Lisa. It can be especially difficult for spouses. They may have jobs at home that they can't leave. Or they may not be permitted to work in the country where the officer is posted. Lisa's husband was lucky: he was able to get a job in Tel Aviv. "It was still very hard to leave my family behind," she says. "In the two years I was there, I was able to go home only once, and that was for my sister's wedding."

Family members left behind can become alarmed by news reports. "My mom called one night, worried about a bombing reported on TV. I reassured her that the incident took place quite far away."

Lisa highly recommends a career in the foreign service. "It's a real commitment of time and energy but I get so much back," she says. "I've already done and seen more things than I ever thought I would. It's really exciting to be working on issues that other people only read about in a newspaper."

Tel Aviv, Israel, where Lisa lived for two years.

Choosing the foreign service can put a strain on family life. "Either you ask your family to pack up and move with you, or you leave them behind for two to five years. On the other hand, what an education for children — to live all over the world."

Career planning

Talk to your teachers and school counselor. Let them know you're interested in a foreign service career. Ask them to suggest materials about other countries for you to read.

Check the phone book to see if there are any embassies or consulates from other countries in your area. Call and ask for information. Ask to interview a foreign service officer.

Making Career Connections

Write to the federal government and request information about entering the foreign service.

Do you have access to the Internet? Look for bulletin boards on a country you are interested in. Look for an international pen pal.

Getting started

Interested in becoming a foreign service officer? Here's what you can do now.

1. Try to get involved in an exchange program through your school. Even if you cannot travel to another country yourself, hosting a foreign student will give you experience relating to people from different cultures.
2. Join a language club at school. You can practice speaking that language and learn more about other cultures.
3. Read newspaper stories about politics, the world, and foreign policy. Find out what is happening and why.
4. Keep a stamp collection. Countries use postage stamps to share events and information with the rest of the world.
5. Study a wide range of subjects in high school, including geography, history, politics, and languages.

Related careers

Here are some related careers you may want to check out.

Translator
Provides written or verbal translations of different languages. Employed by businesses, governments, and publishers.

Cultural anthropologist
Researches human culture and traditions, both current and historical. May teach at the post-secondary level or work as a consultant.

Airline worker
Pilots and flight attendants travel the world as part of their job. Between flights, they are able to see many different areas of the world.

Foreign correspondent
Works for newspapers, wire services, radio, or television. Finds out what is happening in a particular part of the world and reports the news.

Future watch

Advances in communication and travel make the world more accessible to everyone. Relations with other countries are becoming more important, and so is the role of the foreign service officer. In many countries, foreign service officers are actively working toward world peace. They help emerging countries develop by promoting international trade. "As we move toward a global economy with more international trade," Lisa concludes, "I see a growing need for foreign service officers to help businesses and governments."

Crys Mantas — Probation Officer

When someone is convicted of breaking the law, the judge orders some type of "consequence" or punishment. Probation officer Crys Mantas's job is to make sure the judge's orders are carried out. She works with kids between 12 and 15 years old, helping them stay out of trouble.

"A probation officer is a combination social worker and police officer," Crys explains. "Some clients I can talk with and try to help. With others I just have to lay down the law."

Punishment or second chance?

"My clients are offenders who are referred to me after they are found guilty and sentenced by a judge," says Crys. These offenders are not sentenced to jail terms. Instead, the judge has put them on probation. The probation order states the "consequence" that each offender must do to make up for the offense, such as community service, a curfew, holding down a job, regular visits to a probation officer, or regular school attendance. "The judge gives these sentences when there is a good chance that the person can change his or her behavior while remaining in the community."

Crys knows how important this chance is for her clients. "If they don't do what the judge has ordered, they may go back to court. The judge may give them a more severe

consequence, such as jail," she explains. "That's why I do my best to reason with my clients, to keep them focused on succeeding."

Preparing reports

Crys serves the court as well as her clients. "I often write a 'pre-disposition report' about an offender's background." The judge requests this report after finding the person guilty of a crime, but before passing a sentence. To prepare her report, Crys interviews the youth and his or her family members, victims, and teachers. "Sometimes there are family or personal problems," she says. "The judge wants to know all about this person before handing down the sentence."

Dealing with problems

Crys also works with young people who may have emotional problems or substance abuse problems. Dealing with these problems is not always easy.

"I help my clients learn to meet personal goals, such as attending school, while they meet the terms of their probation," Crys says.

"My heart just goes out to some kids," she admits sadly. "When I first started this job it was difficult not to get emotionally involved. But that was hard on my own family. Now, I try to remember that it's their problem, not mine. I can't solve their problems for them." She nods firmly. "But I can help them figure out how to solve their own problems."

With the stress and hardships come great rewards. "It's frustrating when I see kids getting into further trouble," Crys says. "But I know I've helped kids turn their lives around — and that's a tremendous satisfaction."

Getting started

1. Volunteer to be a peer helper at your school. Helping someone identify their problems and find ways to solve them is good experience.
2. Take a course to become a minor sports official, such as a referee or umpire.
3. Visit a court room and watch a trial. Knowledge of the law is crucial for a probation officer.
4. Study a wide range of subjects in school including law, history, and communications.

Robin Duke — Law Clerk

"I help lawyers prepare for their cases," law clerk Robin Duke explains. There is usually too much to be done for the lawyer to manage alone. "My job includes interviewing clients, filing papers at court, or doing research in the law library. And my day can change quickly! I might start by finding files on one case, then have to drop everything to file a document at court. When the lawyers need my help, they usually need it right now."

Preparing for a trial involves a team of people. "Big cases involve several lawyers, legal secretaries, and law clerks," notes Robin. "We're all committed to the same goal: winning the case."

A sea of paper

One of Robin's main responsibilities is paperwork. Every piece of information must be accurately organized and catalogued. "A legal case involves a lot of paperwork.

Paperwork is a big part of Robin's job. "I've had a case last as long as five years," she says, "so you can imagine the mountains of forms, files, and legal opinions!" The use of computers and electronic filing systems is helping to make such information easier to manage.

Some of it has to be filed with the court at the right place and at the right time. If it isn't, the case could be jeopardized." Robin grins. "It helps that I'm a neat freak. I like getting things organized so that everything's right at my fingertips."

Up close and personal

Another part of Robin's job is interviewing clients to get their side of the story. "Sometimes it's stressful," she admits. "You have to ask personal questions. And some of the clients are emotional, which is perfectly understandable. They wouldn't be involved in a legal action unless something important — their families, livelihood, or reputations — were at stake." Based on the interview, she finds out what legal work needs to be done. "We may even discover how to resolve the case without going to court."

When there's work to be done

Being a law clerk can be hectic. "When we have an important case that's about to go to court, we don't work by the clock. We work until we're finished," Robin says. The pressure can become overwhelming. "There have been times when I've realized I had 60 hours of work left to do, and only 48 hours to do it."

Despite the pressure, Robin likes what she does. "I look forward to going to work. The law fascinates me, and each new case is different enough to be interesting." Being a law clerk isn't for everyone, she cautions. "I have to work very hard. But I know I'm part of a team. When we succeed in a case, we celebrate our success together!"

Oldest case

Imagine the problems of handling documents written almost 700 years ago. That's what law clerks in Great Britain had to do recently. The controversy over who should be in charge of Durham Cathedral first flared up in 1283. This issue has been in and out of the courts ever since. The latest attempt to settle matters was unsuccessful, since neither side would accept the documents presented by the other.

Getting started

1. Find out how your family stores and organizes its legal documents. What kinds of information are recorded?
2. Watch a court case on television. Most of the paperwork the lawyers use would have been prepared by a law clerk. (Keep in mind that what you see was produced or edited for television.)
3. Practice using a computer to do research. Try the Internet, too!
4. Think about how you store your school notes. How could you organize them so you could find specific information next year?

Rob Pattison — Lawyer

Lawyers provide legal advice and services to individuals and businesses. Rob Pattison specializes in law that deals with buildings and their construction. "Most people see a lawyer when they buy a house, write a will, or need help to settle a family dispute," Rob says. "But lawyers do many other things. Many, like me, deal with businesses."

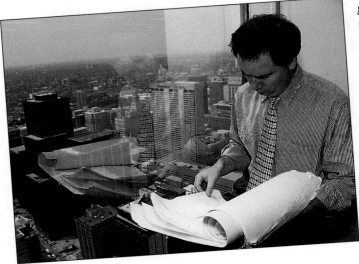

Rob specializes in the legal aspects of the construction industry.

The building business and the law

Rob specializes in working with the construction industry. "Where does the law come in?" he says. "Just about everywhere!" For example, municipal governments set legal requirements for buildings. "Contractors and owners bring me their contracts to check," Rob explains. "I make sure that what they've planned is legal."

Another important part of Rob's legal practice is dealing with disputes after the building has been completed. "One case I recall involved a roof that was not secured properly to the building. The home owner wanted to have it fixed, but didn't know who was responsible for fixing the problem. Was it the contractor who built the roof, the contractor who built the walls, or the architects and engineers who supplied the drawings?" Rob helped determine who should pay. "That's a typical case for me."

Law in the real world

Rob's days usually start around 8:00 in the morning and don't end until 7:00 at night. "Long hours are usual in this profession," he says. "Sometimes the work can be unpredictable. I've worked really late and have even stayed up all night to finish something that had to be done right away."

"When most people think of lawyers, they think about them pleading cases in a court room. Most lawyers spend very little time in court. I do about 90 percent of my work at the office."

A tough road

Becoming a lawyer is a long process. "First, you have to earn a bachelor's degree," explains Rob. "This can be in any subject you like, but many select a field that will help them as lawyers." For example, a person interested in environmental law might choose science. If you obtain good grades during your undergraduate education, you then take the Law School Admission Test. The LSAT is a six hour exam. "Law schools use it to see if you can think like a lawyer."

"Once you finish three years of law school, the training varies. In some places, you can write the 'bar exam' immediately. This is a test given by the law society. Once you pass, you can practice law. In other places, you have to serve an apprenticeship for a year or two before taking your bar exam. Both systems have advantages. With the first one, you can get right to work. The second one gives you more time to prepare for the bar exam and get some experience."

Despite the long hours and pressure-filled days, Rob says he really enjoys his job. "It's fascinating work," he smiles, "and it can be very satisfying. Sometimes I'll drive by a subdivision that I did the legal work on and I'm proud that I had a part in it."

Getting started

1. Visit the guidance office and ask for information on the requirements to enter law school.
2. Do some research into the building laws in your community.
3. You will need good marks to enter law school. Visit each of your teachers and ask for advice on improving your study habits.

Ken McGraw — Speech Writer

Do your friends pay attention to what you say? Do you find you are asked to speak for your group in school? Maybe you could become a speech writer like Ken McGaw. Ken works for a federal politician. "Everyone knows that politicians make a lot of speeches," he explains. "But most people don't realize that these speeches are usually prepared for the politician by a professional speech writer." This is because many politicians don't have time to do their jobs as well as write good speeches. "I take what they want to say and put it into a speech."

Styling a speech

Ken and the other members of the politician's staff meet once a week to review the speaking engagements for the politician and the issues to be discussed. The audience is important. "I wouldn't write the same speech for an agricultural convention as I would for a political rally," Ken notes, "even when the issues and opinions are the same."

Before he sits down to write, Ken may also meet with the politician or policy experts. "The policy experts keep in touch with what's going on in an area," explains Ken. "I count on them for information of interest to the audience to include in the speech."

Ken feels comfortable writing for his current employer. "You get to know a person's style and what he or she likes to emphasize. The speeches I write should sound natural, as though the person were talking to you directly."

Once he knows what to include, Ken goes to work. "I write at least two speeches a week and sometimes quite a few more," he says. "The pace can get quite busy."

Getting there — indirectly

Ken didn't set out to become a speech writer, although he liked writing. After high school, he studied psychology before deciding to get a

Ken researches every fact he includes in the speeches he writes. "The person saying the speech depends on me to be accurate and up-to-date."

degree in journalism. "I worked briefly as a journalist," he recalls. "Then I landed a job working for a political party in the communications department." His job there included writing letters, memos, brochures, newsletters, and — eventually — speeches.

"I recommend that anyone interested in this career should understand communications and the political issues first," says Ken. "That can take some time. You have to be interested in the issues and you have to spend a lot of time reading and learning the background to what is happening." He smiles. "One of the best parts of this career is hearing a good speaker deliver the words I've written, and seeing the audience respond."

Spoken history

Some speeches have become part of history. Look in a book of quotes for lines from famous speeches. Choose a quote that interests you and find out more about the issues that led to this speech.

Getting started

1. Join a public speaking or debating club at school.
2. If you hear a speech or read about a speech that interests you, write to that person and ask for a copy. What made it a good speech?
3. Watch someone making a speech. Listen to the messages that the speaker is trying to get across.
4. In high school, take English, history, politics, and computer training.

Classified Advertising

Help Wanted

PLASTERER/CARPENTER/ PAINTER required for historical renovations. Min 5 yr experience. References required. Send resumé to Joe's Times, 982 Knab St., Arundel, Province/ State, Postal/Zip Code

COURT REPORTER FOR LAW COURTS IN REMOTE AREA. Qualified and certified reporter with some exams. All office support provided. Good salary and transcript fees. Call Joe Shymanski at Northern Employment Services Ltd., 555-1030

Sci-Connections

Sci-Connections is a world leader in providing top-of-the-line equipment to the cable television and tel... industries. We currently have the foll...g opportunities:

DESIGN ENGINEER
Ideal candidate will have a BSEE ...d 5-10 years experience with ...tal telephony, DATACOM, 68... Micro Processor and ... Experience with ACE+ or ...ilar design ... tools and solid knowle... of ... Assembly programm... languages is ... ferred.

TELEPHONY INTERFACE ENGINEER
Position req...s ... (MSEE pre...ed) ... 7+ years ...erienc... analog and ...ital de... related to ...ctronics ... telephony ...e int... application... m... ETSI/ANSI ...ecif... Microproces... design... rience also re...red.

SOFTWARE E...
Ideal candi... ... BSEE or B...

FLIGHT ATTEND...
experienced, for a large ... established company's private ... corporate jet. Totally bilingual in Spanish & English, also Chinese & Russian an asset. Fax resumé to 555-4618

PLASTERS/ACRYLIC FINISHERS —
Experienced only need apply. Call 555-7800, ask for Ross.

SAUSAGE
maker req'd. immed. Must have diploma in food services & min. 3 yrs. exp. 555-7358.

CONTEMPORARY COMMERCIAL ART GALLERY
SALES & MARKETING POSITION
to work with owner and staff organizing openings, developing promotional material, prospecting sales, research projects and much more. We are looking for a career-oriented person with a visual art degree and experience in a creative entrepreneurial environment. If you have excellent people and communication skills, enjoy working with artists, curators and exclusive clientele, are high energy and very hard-working, we want to talk to you. Salary commensurate with experience. **Reply by Sept 19 to Box 3000, Local Star, Mapleton, Province/State.**

METAL FABRICATOR for rust repair/customizing ...otor vehicles. Must be skilled ...making auto panels. Own to... req. Fax resumé; 555-238...

CRU...E SHIP JOBS! ...ear rou... positions. Hiring ...th men...men. Free room & ...ard. Wi...ain. Call, 24 hrs, ...5-7778.

...N 80 b... seniors home ...require... Food Service ...supervi...r/Chef live-in. ...wen... country living. ...re...mé to 555-5564.

...stablished restaurant ...g creative kitchen per... 2 positions available, ...De Partie & Jr Sous ...Send resumés to 34 ...Street, Gardenia City, Province/State, Postal/Zip Code

...mmunicati... is a lea...

WANTED - SOCCER REFEREES

Westville Minor Soccer League needs a teenage referee for the summer. The successful applicant must be reliable, physically fit, and hard-working; know the rules and regulations of soccer; and understand the importance of those rules. Referee training and certification will be provided. Our referees officiate at least five regular games each week, and are expected to travel for tournament games.

Send resumé to:
Kathy St. Martin
Westville Minor Soccer League
555 Brock Street, Westville
Postal/Zip Code

...euner Servi...es Unlimited
...ior Paralegal/Law Cl...

You wi...provi...kately assistance to corporate lawyers handling a variety of legal matters including diverse projects, the day-to-day flow of documents and information, and the development and administration of control systems and procedures.

The successful candidate will have a bachelor's degree/equivalent. Paralegal/Law Clerk training and Certificate required. Must have a minimum of four (4) years of Paralegal/Law Clerk work experience. Excellent research and writing skills as well as strong organizational, human relations and communication skills are required.

We offer our employees an excellent starting salary and an exceptional benefits plan which includes vision/dental/medical coverage, and a generous pension plan. Please send your resumé in confidence to:

CSU, Personnel Department, 4390 Parkwood East, Suite 392, Missangi, Province/State, Postal/Zip Code.

Who got the job?

Finding a job

- Talk with family, friends, and neighbors, and let them know what jobs interest you.

- Respond to "Help Wanted" ads in newspapers.

- Post an advertisement of your skills on a community bulletin board.

- Register at government employment offices and private employment agencies.

- Contact potential employers by phone or in person.
- Send out inquiry letters to companies and follow up with phone calls.

A job application usually consists of a letter and a resumé (a summary of your experience, including volunteer work, as well as your qualifications for the job). Applicants whose resumés show they are qualified may be invited to a job interview.

Activity

Getting a summer job

The advertisement shown on the opposite page, for a soccer referee, was placed in the local paper in early spring. In many communities, summer jobs are hard to find. For a job like this, there might be many applicants who send letters and resumés, but only a few would be granted interviews.

Two of these applicants were Lisa Fiore and Tony Lam. Their letters and resumés, and the notes made by Kathy St. Martin during the interview, are shown on pages 46 and 47.

Procedure

Make a list of the qualifications that you think are important for a good referee. Now consider each applicant's resumé, covering letter, and performance during the job interview. Which candidate has the best qualifications and experience?

Whom do you think Kathy St. Martin should hire for the job: Lisa or Tony? What else, besides qualifications and experience, did you consider in making your decision?

Challenge

How would you perform in a job interview? Role-playing can give you practice in asking and in answering questions. Ask a friend to take the role of Kathy St. Martin and interview you for the job. Then reverse roles. This practice can help make sure that when you apply for a job, you have a good chance of getting it!

Lisa Fiore's application and interview

12 Davidson Avenue
Westville, Province/State
Postal/Zip Code

May 29, 19—

Westville Minor Soccer League
555 Brock Street, Westville
Postal/Zip Code

Dear Ms. St. Martin:

I would like to apply for the position of soccer referee that I saw advertised in the Westville Star.

Before moving here, I played soccer with the Harriston Minor Soccer League. In my last year, my team won the division championship.

The past two summers I worked as an office clerk at my father's real estate office. I have good communications skills and a lot of experience dealing with people.

I have enclosed my resumé for your consideration. Please call me at 555-1513 to arrange an interview.

Sincerely,

Lisa Fiore

Lisa Fiore

Interview: Lisa Fiore

- *Spoke at great length about her years playing soccer. Familiar with most common rules.*
- *Dressed casually — jeans, sweater, and cowboy boots.*
- *When asked how she would handle a confrontation with an adult coach, said she would refer the coach to the league representative.*
- *Plans to study physical therapy at college.*
- *Did not ask any questions about the training or the game schedule.*

Resumé
Lisa Fiore
12 Davidson Avenue
Westville, Province/State
Postal/Zip Code

Education
19— - 19—
Westville High School (one year remaining to graduation) Subjects taken include Business Studies, Office Procedures, English, Art

Work Experience
19— Present
Fiore Real Estate, Westville, Province/State: Duties include answering the phone, greeting clients, and delivering paperwork.

19— Present
Babysitting: I have four regular clients.

Interests
Sports (member of high school soccer, hockey, and basketball teams) Art

References
Available on request

Tony Lam's application and interview

255 Baskerville Circle
Apt. 205
Westville, Province/State
Postal/Zip Code

May 29, 19—

Westville Minor Soccer League
555 Brock Street, Westville
Postal/Zip Code

Dear Ms. St. Martin:

Please accept the enclosed resumé as application for the position of soccer referee.

I have never played soccer, but I am on the high school football and wrestling teams, and I am an assistant ski coach for novice skiers.

As a volunteer at St. Luke's Breakfast Club, I work with young children. I am a hard worker, reliable, and willing to learn.

Thank you for taking the time to consider me for this job. If you would like me to come in for an interview, please call me at 555-3848.

Sincerely,

Tony Lam

Tony Lam

Interview: Tony Lam

- *Dressed neatly — shirt, dress pants.*
- *At first, he answered most questions quietly and with very short answers — often just yes or no. Later he opened up a bit more.*
- *Understands the rules of football and wrestling, has studied soccer rules from a library book, and showed a good working knowledge.*
- *When asked how he would handle a confrontation with an adult coach, said he would check the details in a rule book.*
- *Asked about the game schedule because he cuts grass for several neighbors in the summer.*

Resumé
Tony Lam
255 Baskerville Circle
Apt. 205
Westville, Province/State
Postal/Zip Code

Objective
To work in finance in international business.

Work Experience
Volunteer, St. Luke's Breakfast Club
Duties: Helping one day a week preparing and serving breakfast to school-age children. I also send out letters for donations and update mailing lists on the computer.
Assistant ski coach
Duties: For past ski season, I worked with novice skiers, instructing them on proper conduct and safety as well as technique.

Education
Will graduate this June from Westville High School.
Best subjects: Accounting, History.
Awarded partial scholarship to Brock Business College, Greenville, Province/State.

Interests
History: member of history club for four years
Sports

References: On request

320
MAL

MADISON MEDIA CENTER

Great careers for people

028022

DATE DUE
